CULTIVATING ABANDONED DEVOTION FOR JESUS SERIES

studies in the
BOOK OF JONAH

A Call to Radically Align our Hearts
with God's Global Purpose.

Ryan Shaw

Studies in the Book of Jonah: A Call To Radically Align Ourselves With God's Global Purposes
By Ryan Shaw

Published by IGNITE Media
Global Mission Mobilization Initiative (GMMI)
100 County Rd. 263
Armstrong, MO 65230
(660) 273-2531
www.GlobalMMI.net

ISBN: 978-0-9852314-2-2

All Scripture quotations are taken from the New King James Version. Copyright 1982, Thomas Nelson, Inc.

Cover Design by Tsh Oxenreider and Brianne Brassea

2021 Print
More copies of this writing can be ordered from www.GlobalMMI.net or by contacting info@GlobalMMI.net

Ryan Shaw can be personally contacted at rshaw@globalmmi.net

GlobalMMI.NET

Contents

I. Starting Our Journey...An Introduction

Deep in the heart of every human being resides a self-centered tendency toward what is known, understood and comfortable. Due to our fallen nature, our bent is naturally toward self, its concerns, its preservation and its desires. As followers of Jesus Christ, however, we have been born again and redeemed before the Living God. The finished work of Jesus' death, burial, resurrection and ascension to the right hand of God paves the way for us to live in victorious triumph over proneness to self. While in this world, it is our responsibility to daily work out (or proactively receive) His finished work through purposefully choosing to listen, obey and follow the commands of God and the leading of the Spirit.

The incessant pull to slip back into self-centered living is impossible to overcome apart from Jesus. A consistent, day-by-day, posturing in Him allows our spirits to be bolstered with spiritual vibrancy and sensitivity as we consistently set our naturally cold hearts before the flame of His all consuming fire. This is how we guard against falling into spiritual dullness. God knows our natural propensity toward evil and rebellion and has deliberately (and at the highest cost) made a way to flee it and walk in the glorious resources of heaven to live a radical lifestyle of loving and serving God with all of our hearts.

As the Church of Jesus today is poised for great exploits in the work of proclaiming the Gospel among all peoples, it is critical that we more fully embrace Jesus' call. Not in word only as is common (most of us dutifully ascribe to these things in at least word) but also in thought and action. To do so means we inevitably come face-to-face with many of our deep-seated prejudices, outlooks and perspectives toward those who are different from us. Surrendering to Jesus' leadership in seeing the fulfillment of the Great Commission is the great purpose for why the Church exists. We are not an exclusive "bless me" or "holy" club. Instead, we exist first and foremost to love and enjoy intimate fellowship with God and then to serve others.

What does this have to do with Jonah? The experiences of Jonah are an invitation to go deep with God in allowing Him to eradicate bias and hatred from our heart that we presently might not admit (or even realize). As true believers in Jesus we are not of this world and don't live for its ends. Instead, a deep love and desire for the eternal welfare of others overtakes us and begins to motivate us because of our response to God's love for us. Allowing such a shift within us will affect every arena of our individual life as well as that of our church and ministry. Fervent prayer will increase as the truth of God's passionate love for all is imparted. Giving will be multiplied exponentially as the revelation of why the church exists and how to truly steward God's resources invades our heart. Our priorities will change as we deliberately align our heart with His.

Jonah's experiences cut to the very core of our heart. It is a straightforward book with few options for interpretations. Yet it lays out more than any other Old Testament book the clear plans of God to reach all peoples with His glorious kindness and love, and confronts us with the greatest barrier to seeing His will accomplished – ourselves!

II. How to Use This Study

There is no right or wrong way to use this study. There are a multitude of options of how to make it the most useful to you, the reader. It can be used by an individual or in a group setting, with a group facilitator guiding the discussions.

My suggestion for gleaning the most spiritually is to use the following pattern: Before reading any part of the verse by verse studies, read the Bible portion being studied as a whole (ie: the book of Jonah) at least once. If possible, do this in one sitting. Then read through each verse by verse section, reading each of these Scriptures at least once and maybe twice, before considering the study notes.

As you read through each section of scripture and the study notes, ask the Holy Spirit to speak to you about specific insights and truths He wants to communicate to you. When applicable turn the scripture into prayers. Thank the Lord for the promises you find in the scripture and receive these for your own life. The Lord is ready to meet and draw you into deeper fellowship with Himself through your studies. Invite Him to commune and abide with you in your study. Do not be in a hurry. Set aside plenty of time to spend seeking the Lord and enjoying Him. Drink of the Lord's goodness and bask in His presence. Journal your prayers and write down insights and ideas that the Spirit gives to you. Let your heart be moved to awe at God and to worship Him throughout this process.

The study follows the following format:

- Each passage of Scripture is followed by a brief summary. This overview provides a glimpse into what is taking place in the specific passage and lays out background information.

- Points of insight from the passage are found under the title headings. These points will help you grasp the depth of each passage and challenge you. Pray through each point and consider its application in your life.

- Other Scriptures have been provided to cross-reference various concepts and principles.

- Additional reflection questions delve further into the passage's intention and its relevance individually and to today's global church.

III.   Why Study the book of Jonah?

The book of Jonah is critical to the body of Christ today. It is a powerful little book which, if rightly engaged, has the capacity to impact and transform our lives in a multitude of areas. God is preparing His Bride to reap a massive global harvest of peoples from every tribe, tongue, and nation under heaven. To do so our hearts must be delivered from our wrong ways of thinking about God, ourselves and these peoples. The book of Jonah is an 'onramp' to align our hearts rightly with God's own in this pivotal hour of the Church's history globally.

A)   About More Than A Fish!!!

First, it is critical to give up distracting concerns about the fish itself. The book of Jonah has become shrouded and minimized to a debate of how big the fish might have been, how Jonah survived in the belly of a whale for three days and if the story ever really happened or is mere symbolism. The primary purposes of the book have been overlooked and missed as a result. This book is more than a children's big fish story. We need to get past the Sunday School notions and be ready to receive the powerful message the Lord wants to impart through it. The Jonah story confronts our bigotries and invites us to dream the impossible of seeing God's purposes among hostile people groups accomplished. See the intent of Jonah's story as the Holy Spirit's scalpel to remove our wrong ways of viewing God, His church and the world. Let the Holy Spirit test and convict through Jonah's experiences as we see in ourselves the struggles that Jonah faced. In response confess all shortcomings and receive Jesus' fresh commission and anointing for service.

B)   Jonah - The Test Book of the Bible

Henrietta Mears, the famous mentor of both Billy Graham and Bill Bright, has called the book of Jonah, "The Test Book of the Bible!" This is because Jonah deeply challenges our faith and calls us to either believe or doubt all that is in it. Mears goes on to say, "Our attitude toward the book of Jonah reveals our attitude toward God and His Word!" Everything in the book demands that we believe in the Supernatural God and trust His Word literally and implicitly. On such belief and trust every person either stands or falls. One who does not believe in a miracle-working God misses the focus of the book. God does intervene in human affairs, He does manipulate nature, He does great things that the mind cannot comprehend (sustaining an individual to live in a fish for three days) in order to teach one man about His heart. This is the very delight of God. He ever seeks to teach us more about Himself and His ways. This often includes mind blowing acts that confirm His involvement with us in dramatic ways.

C) The Two-Fold Purpose of God

We find in the book of Jonah a clear presentation of the two highest priorities in the heart of God. First, God is ever seeking to form His people into the likeness of His precious Son, Jesus. The Father loves the Son more then anything else and seeks to form Jesus' likeness more and more into His bride on earth, the body of Jesus Christ. God's ministry to a person is as important as His ministry through that person. He often does this through adversity. What and who we are is fundamental to what we do. In the book of Jonah, God is concerned as much with the change He wants to bring to Jonah as the change He wants to bring to Nineveh.

Second, God is in passionate pursuit of accomplishing His purpose of restoring a broken and hurting world. This purpose, first laid out through His covenant with Abraham, is to bless nations through the people of God. In the book of Jonah God has mercy upon Nineveh because they responded to His message in spite of God's flawed vessel. This was a whole city that did not know its left hand from its right. This meant that they had no understanding of the Living God or His ways of salvation and restoration.

Much of the world today could be categorized in this group. They are blindly living for self with no idea of what is to come or the accountability they will one day be required to face before the throne of God. They have no idea of the life that was intended for them to live before the foundations of this world. The fall brought complete confusion to what life is about. Through the cross and resurrection, restoration to God's initial plan for life can be again realized.

D) Implementing a Dramatic Paradigm Shift

During the reign of Jeroboam II, Israel possessed a growing perverse attitude concerning Jehovah. She thought that God created her for Him alone and that God's perspective toward outsiders was only hatred, contempt and hostility. In Jonah we find a representation of the common attitude of pride surrounding God's chosen people. God's full and correct outlook for the surrounding peoples (and all peoples) seen through His divine pity, His divine patience, His divine power is clearly revealed as we consider His dealing with Jonah. Vicariously our own attitudes are challenged and we are called to receive the impartation of the Holy Spirit that aligns our heart with God's white-hot Message Bearer passions! Jesus' body feels the sting of the indictment of allowing ourselves to be bent on being merely a "bless me" club instead of the "city on a hill" which we are called to be.

E) Understanding God's Message Bearer Heart

The book of Jonah more then any other in the Old Testament portrays God's zeal for all peoples, no matter how hostile or opposed to His heart they may be. This grand purpose of Almighty God, which dates back to His promise to Abraham of blessing all the nations through Israel, is the focal point of this book. The book of Jonah is meant to teach the body of Christ today the absolute inclusiveness of God's Kingdom through Jesus Christ and to rebuke our propensity and attitude of being an exclusive people.

We find much about the character of God in the book of Jonah. We see His immense compassion toward peoples outside Israel and His special dealings with those who call upon His name. We also find His great passion to bring about "the impossible" by moving in power and literally seeing an entire unreached city brought to repentance.

We are called to dream big through this book, turn from small hopes and welcome the Spirit of God to cultivate within us a global vision of hearts turning en masse and being found in Jesus Christ. A global harvest of incredible proportions is coming as we near the end of the current Church age. This is a promise from God and is meant to provide us with encouragement and confidence in the midst of our present circumstances.

F) Understanding the Ways of God in Shaping His People

In Jonah's story we are meant to grasp some of the ways which God will use to shape and train His children. We study Jonah in order to be aware of the sovereign hand of God moving and teaching us through potentially similar means. God brings about a powerful paradigm shift (noted above) in His prophet. It is critical to see how He does this so we can see the same work taking place in ourselves and help others recognize it. God brought to Jonah four items which were used to shape him:

1) A ministry assignment

2) A challenge to obedience that he ultimately failed

3) A negative occurrence due to this disobedience, designed to draw him back

4) A repeated obedience challenge that was passed and resulted in blessing.

As Jonah reflected on this process, God challenged him to see things from His own perspective, bringing about the paradigm shift.

G) Jonah – A Type of Israel

We see Jonah as a representation of Israel. In several portions Jonah is also to be seen as a type of Christ Himself. But the connection as a type of Israel is astounding. Jonah was called by God to go outside of his own people; so was Israel. Jonah refuses to engage and obey this great calling; so did Israel. Jonah is punished through being thrown into the raging sea; Israel is disciplined by God by being scattered among the nations. Jonah is preserved; so is Israel. Jonah repents to God and is spit out of the fish and restored to life and his calling; Israel will be thrown out of all the nations and one day restored to her former position of greatness. Jonah, now obedient to God, goes ahead with God's commission; Israel, eventually in obedience to Jesus, will become a witness in all the earth. Jonah's ministry is blessed by God in that Nineveh is brought to repentance; Israel will be blessed through the great harvest which will come within and without her.

IV. Who Was Jonah?

Since many critics of this powerful little book see Jonah as a fictitious character, it is important to lay out clear historical fact and background about this man. Jonah was from a town called Gath-Hepher, about an hour north of Nazareth. He lived during the kingly reign of Jeroboam II and is the same "Jonah" that is referenced in 2 Kings 14:25. He aided Jeroboam, making his kingdom powerful and prosperous. Jonah was a statesman for the Northern Kingdom of Israel. It is very probable that Jonah was among the leaders of Elisha's "schools of the prophets." He was a disciple of Elisha and succeeded him as a prophet.

Secondly, it is imperative that we understand the narrative itself to be historical and true and not mere fiction. There is nothing whatsoever in the writing itself to suggest that it is to be understood as fiction and not a factual record of events. Tradition itself suggests that the Hebrews never questioned its true historical accuracy. The early Christian Church emphatically upheld its historical significance.

There was no Biblical representation more used in the underground catacombs of the Roman Empire then that of Jonah. These believers clung to their faith that the resurrection of the saints was very real and Jonah's depiction in the deep enflamed such faith. The Church Fathers (Jerome, Iraneous, Augustine, Chrysostom) all believed in the historical reality of the book as did the Reformers (Calvin, Luther and Zwingli). Most importantly Jesus Himself confirms it is fact as He refers to the story of Jonah several times in His own preaching. Jesus even compares Jonah's experience in the whale as a type of what He will soon suffer. The more recent questioning of the historical actuality of the book of Jonah has only been by those in the rationalistic school of thought who seek to explain away the supernatural realities of the book.

The Book of Jonah – Passage 1

READ Jonah 1:1-3 - Jonah's Call and Response

Jonah is identified as the same prophet of the Northern Kingdom from 2 Kings 14:25. He receives a clear call from God to go to Nineveh. He is to cry out against it or prophesy of what is to come if they do not turn from their wicked and pagan ways. Their perversion and wickedness had arisen before God and the bowls of filth were full and required justice. The call causes Jonah to literally run the other way and flee the situation entirely; in doing so he is trying to get away from God.

A)   The Great City

Nineveh was great! God was not sending His prophet to a place of insignificance. It had immense importance in the ancient world and was situated on the Tigris River about 400 miles from the Mediterranean Sea. It was the capital city of Assyria. Its appearance was incredible, possessing five walls (each 100 feet high) and three moats around it. The walls were thick enough for four chariots to ride on top of them side by side. It had a huge population (more then 600,000 people) who were in complete spiritual darkness. The Ninevites were a brutal and cruel people who oppressed multitudes of people groups including the Israelites. Their war tactics were tortuous and they brought great destruction on all they attacked.

B)   God's Relentless Mercy

To cry out against Nineveh was to prophesy that trouble and disaster was coming. God's compassion was clearly manifested in His call to "cry out against it." His desire was to bring a solution to bear that would protect them from inevitable judgment that was necessary for justice to be realized. In the same way, God loves those today who are outside of a relevant hearing of Christ's Gospel in a way they can culturally grasp and respond to. God longs for them to experience His greatness, His salvation and His deliverance from the power of sin and the evil one. God longs to restore them to the fullness of life that was intended for them to live from the foundations of the world.

Our call is to proclaim the great trouble and disaster that awaits those who do not repent of their sin and believe in the power of the shed blood of Jesus Christ. This is obviously an eternal trouble yet has a correlating trouble in the present. In time, justice for wickedness must come to pass in the here and now and the only protection from such judgment is the precious blood of the Lamb.

In this particular situation the time for judgment had come and God, in His relentless mercy, seeks to send His message bearer to call for a turning of hearts in order to alleviate the required justice.

Such times are coming soon upon many nations, peoples and systems of the world. Wickedness has ascended before God and justice must be satisfied. God's desire is always mercy before judgment yet He will never force any person, city, nation or system to pursue His mercy. We choose this as a result of our will becoming activated.

Reflection Questions:

➢ Is such an understanding of God's calling as a Message Bearer consistent with your current outlook?

➢ How can you welcome the Lord today to bring a paradigm shift regarding His call to help others avert the great disaster coming upon them?

Further Study:
Romans 2:4
Psalm 10:11
Matthew 24:47-51
James 2:13

C) Guarding Against Polluting Mindsets

We are not yet given any reasons why Jonah responded negatively as he did. The prevailing Israelite mindset of the day was that Israel had a corner on God and did not want Him to care for any other people. We see Jonah tainted in this same way.

This is a caution to all who follow God and who lead God's people. We are not above having the wrong outlooks of those around us (in the Christian community) polluting our own hearts and minds. We are called to proactively guard our hearts with the Word of God and the revelation of the Spirit and remain free from the multitude of wrong outlooks and understandings that many buy into. Only an ongoing pursuit of intimacy and increasing fellowship with Jesus keeps us free from this. He is the personified "Word" and reveals to us the deep understanding of the written Word. Apart from consistently seeking Him we will become tainted as Jonah did.

Many in the global Church today possess a similar mindset as the Israelites. We so easily reek of an inward-looking, self-centered, "God is all about me" perspective which is foreign to the heart of the Father. Though He cares immensely for each of us and reveals this through a myriad of unforgettable ways, His purpose is to provoke us to rightly align our outlooks and lives with His own. Jesus was never concerned about His own will, only the will of the Father. As we move from immaturity to maturity in God we find ourselves increasingly concerned with His chief concerns. These are always toward those who are presently outside of His Kingdom, seeking to move them closer to His own heart.

➤ In what areas have you allowed a wrong mindset of God being "all about me" to pollute your thinking? When we're honest we realize that we all have, to some degree. Being aware of it, however, allows us to confess it and receive the Spirit's power to turn from it.

Further Study:
Jeremiah 17:9

Prayer:
Father, I recognize my tendency to easily take on the prevailing mindsets of those in my community, whether or not they are in line with Your Word, ways and commands. I receive Your power by faith to allow the Holy Spirit to mold my thinking and give me a heart which reflects Your greatest desires for all peoples. Forgive me for my self-centered outlook which often acts as if all that matters is myself. Take this heart out of me and replace it with a heart which is aligned with that which is the greatest importance to Your own heart.

D) Escaping the Presence of God

Jonah sought to literally get away from God. There was a false understanding in the ancient world that a god only had authority in the specific places where it was worshipped. Jonah, though a prophet of the Most High God and chosen by His hand, was still human and prone to incorrect theology and practice. Outside of Israel, Jonah believed he could escape God's power.

How often we possess a similar misguided view. Yet ours has a different application. In our Christian culture we believe intellectually that God is everywhere (omnipresent) yet we consume our lives with busyness, entertainment and work-related priorities and subtly tune Him out.

We forget that He has purchased us and has blood-bought rights over every portion of our lives as Lord and Leader. We fail to recognize that His intention for us from the foundation of the world was to enjoy an intimate and close friendship based on trust and dependence. This is what Adam and Eve had with God before the fall and this is what redemption, reconciliation and restoration through Jesus makes available once again to those who will rightly receive it and act upon it.

E) Having a Teachable Spirit

Jonah, though in disobedience, had a teachable heart and God broke through (later in the book) in molding him. Possessing such a heart allowed God to impart a greater measure of understanding and compassion to His servant. A teachable posture is critical to all those whom God will use over a lifetime. In spite of the multitudes of failures in the life of King David, his heart was always teachable.

Many of us have forsaken such a teachable spirit and shut ourselves off to God through our disobedience. The disobedience in itself is not so much a concern to God. It is the response to the knowledge that we have disobeyed that God is mostly watching. When the Lord sends others or orchestrates situations to confront us or help us see an area of disobedience, it is imperative that we quickly confess our disobedience and receive His correction. The tragedy is that many of us are not even aware that we do not possess a teachable heart.

Reflection Questions:

➤ Where is your lifestyle inconsistent with the reality that the gaze of God is constantly upon you?

➤ How can you practically cultivate a greater teachable spirit starting today?

Further Study:
2 Chronicles 16:9
Proverbs 5:21
Proverbs 17:3

F)   Jonah – A National Hero?

In many ways, Jonah possessed the spirit of a national hero of Israel. Consider it for a moment! Assyria was a dreaded enemy of Israel. God speaks to Jonah about going to its capital (Nineveh) to call them to repentance. Such an action could cause them actually to do so and escape the judgment God intended to bring. This would keep them from being destroyed which would potentially continue to endanger Israel as they could rise up later and oppress them once again. By fleeing, Jonah seeks to eliminate the option of the Ninevites repenting and avoiding doom and instead be destroyed by God, protecting Israel from this enemy. Jonah would sacrifice himself for the sake of saving his people, Israel. Yet he was horrendously misguided.

God's ways are not our ways. How often we seek to "help" God because what He seems to be doing doesn't fit with our vision of how victory will come. Remember Abraham who tried to "help" God bring to pass His promise to bring Abraham a son. Instead of depending upon Him to accomplish it according to His all-wise plan, Abraham slept with Sarah's servant Hagar. God's ways will almost always contradict our self-willed plans and purposes. Spiritual maturity leads us to yield and submit to Him even if it confuses, angers or even offends us about God. For in doing so our spiritual lives are being enlarged in God.

Reflection Questions:

➤ When have you sought to help God out in fulfilling His promises to you?

➤ What did He teach you through that experience?

Further Study:
Genesis 16:1-4
Isaiah 55:8-9

Prayer:
Lord, forgive me for justifying my disobedience toward Your leading. I see how often I do what Jonah did. I look at a situation and try to act as if I know better then You. I know that You want to mature me by testing my willingness to follow You even when I don't understand Your leading. You are Lord and I am not!

STUDIES IN THE BOOK OF JONAH   Page 18

The Book of Jonah – Passage 2

READ Jonah 1:4-6 - The God Who Intervenes

In these verses the intentional intervening hand of God is revealed. His authority over created order is in full display as He sends a great wind to stir up the sea. God is orchestrating events in response to the disobedient choice Jonah had made.

A) Called to Christ-likeness

God is committed to shaping and forming His people into the likeness of Jesus Christ. His dealings with Jonah are not so much punishment or discipline but a sign of His mercy to teach Jonah and expand Jonah's perspective on God's ways.

It is one of God's greatest purposes to take us in our weakness and brokenness and, in an ongoing fashion, cleanse us of former ways of thinking and purify wrong thought processes. He does this by breathing the very life of Christ within us through the Holy Spirit when we are born again. He then calls us to allow Jesus' fullness of life to live in us and through us. We do not become like Jesus through mere will power or by trying harder but by dying to self-effort and receiving His very life into every circumstance and over every area of flesh and sin. Jesus has given us every spiritual resource to live a life totally abandoned to Him and walk according to the Spirit. We have the responsibility to receive such resources by faith and believe the reality of "Christ in you, the hope of glory!"

<u>Reflection Questions:</u>

➢ How do you usually view God's discipline of you? When have you recognized it as His mercy and grace to form you into His likeness?
➢ In what ways have you been seeking to be like Jesus through greater self-effort? How did that work out?

<u>Further Study:</u>
Galatians 2:20
Philippians 3:10
Colossians 1:27

B) The Hound of Heaven

Jonah had fallen asleep—either from a state of depression or from sheer exhaustion after his rushed fleeing. The captain calls upon Jonah to pray to his God for help. The Lord is the faithful One who will pursue us in order to beckon us back to Him. He has sometimes been called the "Hound of Heaven" for His relentless pursuit to bring His people back. To do this He must often oppose us in order to open our eyes to something He wants us to see. God is the Lord of all wisdom and knowledge and He knows the best way to get our attention in every circumstance. The only question is whether we will respond to him or turn away. Often the people of God turn away because we do not understand why God has acted in a certain way or allowed something we saw as inconsistent with His character. We get offended at Him and turn further away. We miss His pursuit to bring us back when it comes through Him opposing us in some way, yet this is precisely one of His marvelous ways of getting our attention. He is jealous over us and wants us to trust Him implicitly, though it may look very different than we might expect.

Reflection Questions:

➤ When have you experienced God's opposition in some capacity in order to reveal to you some key lesson He was seeking to teach? What was your reaction?
➤ In what situation were you tempted to rebel against God because He brought such discipline in a way you didn't see as consistent with His character?

C) God is the Orchestrator

The notion that God orchestrates disastrous events in the world is a controversial one today in the body of Christ. We struggle to believe that God would really plan for events that could prove deadly to people. Yet there are multitudes of Biblical examples that teach us otherwise, including this one. God does purposefully orchestrate certain events and at other times allows evil people to fulfill the plans in their hearts. His intentions in doing so are always good and to bring about the change He desires in people. If we align quickly with His heart such disasters could be averted as we will see later with the Ninevites. Yet God will never violate a person's will. If not submitted to, He must continue along the line of bringing the disaster to pass.

We can easily get tripped up in our way with God by becoming overly focused on fleshly compassion. God does want us to take care of the poor and sick and comfort those in trouble. He has called us to let His love for people be our highest motivation. Yet, there are times when He is distinctly seeking to teach or draw an individual or people out through a process of discipline. If we intervene in our fleshly compassion, we could potentially shortchange the process. It is absolutely critical that we seek to grow in the spiritual gift of discernment in order to know when to act and when to stand back and let God have His way. In this situation God was purposefully orchestrating the event in order to bring His wayward servant back to Himself. When this was accomplished, God relented and stopped the disaster.

Further Study:
Isaiah 45:7
Isaiah 31:2

The Book of Jonah – Passage 3

READ Jonah 1:7-9 - Jonah's Declaration

The crew seeks to figure out why the storm is happening to them. They cast lots and it falls on Jonah. Their eyes turn to him and they berate him with questions to understand the situation. Jonah responds with faith, showing that he is beginning to see what is going on.

A) The God Who Is In Control

The crew decides to cast lots to see who the culprit is behind the crisis. Through a strange divination technique, God shows that He is in control of detailed events such as this. It is He who controls the casting of lots, though this cannot be a promise that He will do so each time. But when He chooses, He is able to use anything of His choosing to reveal truth. Even in the hands of unbelievers.

<u>Reflection Questions:</u>

- Do you believe God to truly be coordinating and sovereignly overseeing the intimate details of your life and ministry calling? If not, why not?
- Consider some events in your life where the hand of God was clearly orchestrating circumstances. How did it make you feel?

<u>Further Study:</u>
Psalm 66:7
Daniel 5:21

B) God's Restorative Hand

The crew recognized that someone had done something tremendously wrong. They understood that such circumstances must be a result of divine justice being employed as a result of someone in their midst. Jonah could have told them from the beginning that the situation was his own doing, but he chooses to keep quiet until the lot fell on him. The process of God reclaiming His wayward prophet is outstanding! Jonah begins to buy into the fact that God was indeed after him and seeking him deliberately because of his disobedience. Others on the ship were undoubtedly stained with horrendous sin, yet the whole episode took place because of Jonah.

It is one's own child that a parent disciplines if they have gone astray. The purpose is always to restore and bring back to relationship and obedience. God is willing to go to great lengths to find His lost sons and daughters and bring them back. God will find those who sin against Him, those who desert Him, those who seek their own way instead of His and seek to bring them back. Yet, as we see with Jonah, this is not an easy way. Obedience to God and His will from the beginning is always the easiest way.

Reflection Question:

➤ Do you personally believe that God will go to great lengths to discipline you in order to restore you unto right relationship with Himself?
➤ If so, when specifically did you recognize Him doing this?
➤ What do you think motivates this in Him?

Further Study:
Luke 15:11-32
Proverbs 15:32
Hebrews 12:5-11

C)   Jonah's Declaration

Jonah is berated with questions about what he has done to invite the crisis. The shipmen don't attack him harshly, however, as we might expect. Instead with some compassion, they inquire and seek information regarding who this man was and what his offense had been. What was the grave sin that had brought such a display of divine force? In answering, Jonah simply affirms his nationality and his religious affiliation.

He declares that he fears the Lord, the God he worships, the God he prays to, the God of heaven and the sovereign creator God who makes all and is in control of all. He is not the God of any particular country but He who is over all and in all and through all. In this way, Jonah is coming to a greater understanding that his God is definitely not limited to any geographical area as he had once thought. He also sees that he has not been faithful to trust in the Lordship of God in his life. The declaration is first a condemnation of his own foolishness, and second, a desire to show these men who the one true God really is.

We will all, at some point in our lives, come to such a crossroads as well. God will set up circumstances that open our eyes to the scope of His authority and grandeur in greater detail. He will graciously provoke us to see Him in His fullness and rely upon Him as our all in all. He will call us to surrender our lives to His absolute Lordship and seek no longer to lead or control our lives according to our own will.

➢ When it is revealed to you that a perspective you've held about God is incorrect, what is your response? How could you have responded with humility as Jonah did?

➢ Jonah came to the crossroads where he finally began to see God as He really is in His grandeur and authority. What do you need to do to experience this crossroad if you haven't already?

The Book of Jonah – Passage 4

READ Jonah 1:10-13 - "Why Have You Done This?"

This is a great drama on the high seas. The crew is greatly afraid at what they now know about God and why He has caused this storm to rage. They ask Jonah, "Why have you done this?" They understood that God was angry for the offense that Jonah had committed. They recognized they were a target because he was with them. They might have looked inward with a searchlight, questioning, if a prophet of God is being punished for one seemingly small offense, how much more should we be punished for our great and terrible offenses against this same Almighty God?

A) Bringing Back the Calm

Jonah proposes his own death after the crew inquires of Jonah how to appease his God for such an offense. Jonah is willing to be sacrificed in order that the others on board do not suffer death. Something must be done to calm the raging storm and Jonah and the crew knew it. The sin was discovered and now some payment had to be made to atone for the sin. They all instinctively understood this basic law of nature.

Sin brings hardship and difficulty to one's life and if not confessed and turned from, it grows and brings more and more difficulty until eventually it completely sears the conscience. The storm of sin must be dealt with in order to bring back the calm. It must be detested and put away in order that the calm (peace of God) might return. This is powerful imagery of how sin causes untold storms and problems in the lives of those who tolerate it. Such a way is difficult and produces great pain both to us and to those around us. To embrace Jesus' cross and receive His resurrection victory over the power of sin is a much better and less painful way.

Reflection Questions:

➢ Recall a time when your sin brought about great hardship for yourself and possibly those around you
➢ Where are you tolerating sin in your life? What will you do about it today?

Further Study:
Romans 6:23
Job 11:14
Jeremiah 4:1
Proverbs 13:15

B) The Justice of a Holy God

Justice must be kept by a holy God and this requires a sacrifice for sin. This is a foreshadowing of Jesus' act as the perfect and unblemished sacrificial Lamb of God that satisfies every need for justice and righteousness. Believing in and receiving His sacrifice as the atonement for our sin meets every requirement of justice for sin. Wrapped up in Jesus is every resource necessary to walk rightly with God, receive His holiness in our lives, be fully pleasing to Him, obey His commands, accomplish His purposes, and prepare rightly for His return.

Reflection Questions:

➢ Where are you not availing yourself to all that has been purchased for you through the death, resurrection and ascension of Christ?
➢ How much of God do you really want?
➢ Are you willing to lay aside distractions to seek Him with all your heart?

Further Study:
Philippians 3:12
1 Timothy 6:12
2 Peter 1:3

C) Jonah's Repentance

Through Jonah's own sacrifice, he was asking that this storm might be stopped. It was an admirable offer as it showed a heart of true repentance. He saw that this was a way to submit to God who was causing the storm because of Jonah's own sin. Jonah takes the sin and owns it, fully recognizing God's justified anger in it and that this sin has brought about such discipline. Heart-felt, humbled, meaningful repentance, turning from our ways and the self-life and surrendering ourselves to the mercies of God, is the pathway to all spiritual restoration. Jonah became aware that God, in His mercy, was relentlessly pursuing him and there is no doubt that his heart was moved by such tough love on the part of God.

Such reality, when pressed upon our hearts brings the same results. The severity of God is always motivated by His gracious mercy and love. Such love, experienced in the depths of our hearts, moves us to see our shortcomings from His divine perspective and enables us to confess and turn from the foolishness of our ways, receiving His power and effectual blood to do so. What kindness the Lord reveals to us. Not only does He forgive us of our sin but also provides the very power necessary to break the stranglehold of sin over our weak flesh. We can never find a way out of sin in our own power and might.

Reflection Question:

➢ God's severity toward us is a sign of His extraordinary love for us. Reflect on a time when the Lord was severe with you in a way that clearly revealed His immense love for you.

D) There Must Be Another Way

In response, the crew row toward shore in vain, hoping for a way out of the mess that didn't include killing Jonah. They had come to view Jonah as an honorable man. This made it increasingly difficult for them to consider killing him by throwing him over board. This is a problem as "good" men also are sinners who need atoning for sin. One's perceived goodness or sincerity often keeps them from being brought before the cross, humbled enough to receive the forgiveness of sins and the redemption which God, through Christ, so freely offers. Instead of submitting to God's plans and prescribed manner of atoning for sin (through the shedding of blood) they sought another way.

This is the way of the world. The belief that sin can be dealt with through some other way results in philosophies and entire religions being developed which keep multitudes bound in their deceptive webs. Sin must always be dealt a death blow and God lovingly crushed His only Son as the only satisfactory provision for salvation. Toleration of sin invites God's justice and judgment as it must be atoned for. Not being willing to follow God's prescription of repentance, cleansing through blood and the forsaking of sin, is to invite harsher dealings and more storms in life. We find that the sea grew increasingly rough as the men sought another way.

Reflection Questions:

➢ Recall a time when you were tempted to find "another way" to get free from your sin. Was it effective? What came of such an attempt?
➢ As you consider other people, or the nations, has the lie crept in that somehow they can still be saved apart from believing in the shed blood of Christ?
➢ What will you do about that this week?

Further Study:
Hebrews 9:22
John 14:6
John 10:7-10

Prayer:
Jesus, I see how easy it is to think that there is another way to find cleaning from my waywardness (sin). I ask You to forgive for dong this. It is only through Your shed blood that I can be washed and made new on the inside, free from all of my wrong doing, thinking, motives and more. It is only through Your resurrection power that I can remain free from such pollution in my heart and life. Help me to always point the way to You as the only freedom from the inward darkness that keeps me separated from You!

The Book of Jonah – Passage 5

READ Jonah 1:14-17 - Thrown Into The Sea

The crew is petrified and finally give in and throw Jonah over board. Sin is always difficult to separate ourselves from. We long to hold on, making excuses for it instead of dealing ruthlessly with it. The crew finally submitted to this end and sought God to have mercy on them and not count Jonah's blood against them. They prayed specifically to the God of Israel, recognizing the truth of Jonah's words regarding this great God.

A)   A Startling Contrast

The blood of God's saints is precious to Him and these shipmen recognized that Jonah was a worshipper of the true God. God's vengeance had been released upon Jonah and though God had an issue with Jonah, they did not want the blood of such a saint counted against them.

Consider such a "fear of God" from men who knew nothing about the greatness of God Most High. Contrast this with what was going on simultaneously during the exact same time period among Israel. Israelites were killing God's prophets and shunning the very messengers God was sending to them to correct their way. What a contrast! The supposed people of God didn't recognize those sent to them by God Himself and yet this crew of sinners recognized a true man of God among them. The world often times recognizes the hand of God before believers do.

<u>Further Study:</u>
Psalms 116:15

B)   Jonah's State

The men move toward execution after clearing their own guilt of bloodshed before the one true God. Jonah must have been in a terrible state of mind in that moment. Having just walked in deliberate disobedience and knowing that he was soon to be in the presence of the One from whom he had been fleeing. A trembling thought indeed!

Jonah is to be an example here of what must be done with sin. It is to be abandoned and drowned, completely cut off and never returned to again. We have been called to put sin away as we recognize that it's only end is spiritual death. Such deliberate actions are the onramp toward personal revival.

<u>Reflection Question:</u>

➤ What areas of sin is the Spirit putting His finger on in your life? Don't be tempted to only consider the "gross" sins. How are you doing with bitterness, inner rage, pride, self-centeredness, self-condemnation, self-consciousness, anger, worry, anxiety, fear, unforgiveness, greed, covetousness, thoughtlessness, etc? Make a covenant with the Lord to cut these off from your life. Receive Jesus' power to do so.

<u>Further Study:</u>
Isaiah 55:7
Luke 14:33
Ezekiel 20:8

C)   God's Two-Fold Purpose

We find a two-fold purpose of God in this entire ordeal- dealing with His prophet and revealing Himself to the crew. As soon as Jonah was in the sea, the raging storm broke and all was calm. The sea sought him and when it had him, it relented. God was ordering all of this for His process of transforming the heart and paradigm of His beloved servant. He rules over the seas and the storms and over the natural and physical environment.

This led the shipmen to worship God and fear Him exceedingly with a healthy outlook and perspective. God seeks to bring glory to Himself in all situations and circumstances. His desire is to partner with us in such endeavors and allow us to point to Him as the glorious One that He is. His revelation to the shipmen through this ordeal is startling and we find the beating heart of a love-consumed God for all peoples whom He has created by His hand. No matter what kind of pagan system they are currently held hostage by, God desires them to see Him and worship Him as Lord of heaven and earth.

D)   God's Deliberate Interventions

Though Jonah expected drowning, God was not through with His training of Jonah. He had lessons of transformation and restoration still to come. The shipmen were now saved and the ability of His prophet to flee was now overcome. Yet, Jonah still had not fully grasped the heart of the Father regarding the situation. To help with this understanding, God brings forth a great fish to swallow him. God, again, is seen as completely orchestrating this event. It is not random or haphazard, but deliberate and calculated by God Himself. Jonah is saved by this fish who keeps him from drowning.

Do we see God's hand in our own circumstances? It is critical that we expand our horizons to discern God's handiwork with greater responsiveness in every day life and what the purposes of His heart are in each of them. Events are not as haphazard as we may think. We simply have not learned the skill of discerning God's hand and purposes within them.

➤ Are you regularly able to discern God's hand in your circumstances, either positive or negative? This is a critical ability to develop before the Lord. God is constantly orchestrating circumstances for our sakes yet often we don't perceive what he is doing. A careful study of Biblical characters such as Joseph, Moses, Daniel and many more reveal this ability to be critical.

➤ How will you develop this discernment?

E) The Purpose of the Intervention

Jonah was alive and well inside the fish for three days in order to be protected, that God might reconcile Jonah to Himself. This miraculous intervention was implemented for at least three reasons:

1) As a pillar of God's mercy – In order that all those who have run from Him might return to Him, repent, and receive the full restoration with all the accompanying privileges which God offers His children.

2) That Jonah might successfully go and preach to Nineveh. Such a miraculous testimony of the goodness and severity of God would evidently add to the spiritual authority of his message.

3) As a type of Christ, Jonah was buried and rose again after three days and nights in the fish's belly. His burial was a figure of Christ Himself. Both came forth in order to bring repentance to the gentile world.

The Book of Jonah – Passage 6

READ Jonah 2:1-10 - Jonah's Prayer and Repentance

This passage is Jonah's response to God as he sits in the belly of the whale. It is a powerful prayer, revealing that Jonah understands and grasps the revelation of God and the purpose behind the whole episode. At a heart level, Jonah is returning to his God through ongoing repentance and giving himself unto worship. Thanksgiving erupts from his heart over not being given the death sentence Jonah knew he justly deserved. Relationship with God was broken by Jonah's fleeing and now it was being restored through the cries of Jonah's heart by a kind and all forgiving God.

A) Affliction – God's Vehicle

Affliction is the vehicle God often uses to motivate us to prayer. Instead of standing against affliction in defiance, we ought to let the difficulties, hardships, adversities, pressures and persecutions bring us face to face with God Most High. And to always allow it to do so in a spirit of humility on our part. Though much affliction is self-imposed due to our sin, let us come in contrition and softness of heart before the throne of grace and tenderness as we experience it.

Reflection Questions:

➢ Consider the various hardships and adversities you have experienced. Ask the Lord to speak to you about His intentions through them. What was He teaching you? How was He forming you? Did you receive such as being from Him?

Further Study:
Isaiah 30:20-21
Proverbs 24:10
Ecclesiastes 7:14

B) Communion with Jesus

No geographical place can keep us from communion and fellowship with Jesus. The bottom of the sea in the belly of a fish, this unconventional place became the sacred ground of reconciliation between Jonah and God. No matter the situation or circumstance we find ourselves in we have been provided with open access to God Almighty. We possess the life of Christ dwelling within us and have access to the fullness of the Spirit. This hinges on us coming before Him with a spirit of humility, true brokenness and contrition. We are to see ourselves in light of God Himself and recognize that nothing good dwells in us. Jonah did this and the Lord met with Him in a profound way.

Reflection:

➢ Prayer and worship is the response of a submitted heart in adversity and hardship. Pour your heart out to Jesus asking for power and enabling to always respond in such a way in the midst of adversity and pain.

C) The God Who Answers Prayer

God hears and answers Jonah's cries and does so with us as well. The great God of covenantal love and acceptance, the great One who called Jonah and from whom Jonah fled, is the same God who now answers Jonah's prayers. He shows no partiality among His people and does this for all who come to Him in their weakness and cling to Him alone - no matter our age, gender, ethnicity, education, social status, etc.

When we come to God in the prescribed manner that He has ordained He cannot fail to respond to us. Such a manner includes admitting our folly and sin, recognizing His power over sin through the cross, believing in His authority to bring us into victory and make us right before God the Father and turning from the sin. Seek Him for these things with a true and sincere heart of love and He will answer and restore in the same way He did for Jonah.

Reflection Questions:

➢ Such answers to prayer build our confidence in God. Do you possess absolute assurance that God is for you and has your best interest in mind? Confidence in God is at the core of rightly living a life pleasing unto Him and being used for His glory.
➢ How can you develop or strengthen this confidence?
➢ Have you experienced God lately as the prayer hearing God?

Further Study:
John 14:12-14
Matthew 7:7-12

D) The Greatness of God in Redemption

Through Jonah's prayer, we see that Jonah is ever aware of his guilt and unworthiness before a Holy God. He sees God as acting to pull him from the pit and to give him life when he doesn't deserve it. Jonah had failed to do what God required of His Message Bearers and that is to be faithful and obedient. Yet, God in His unswerving commitment to us is seen as fully pardoning

Jonah and restoring him. We are to marvel at the greatness and love of God in redemption. A Holy God reaching out to a stained and filthy people in order to fully reconcile us to intimacy and deep communion with Himself. This reality should always leave us clinging to humility and our nothingness before Him in His Splendor. What a glorious salvation He has provided for with all of its accompanying blessings and privileges.

Reflections:

➤ Allow your spirit to revel in the magnitude of what God has provided for us through the death and resurrection of His Son.
➤ Ask God for His enabling that your entire life might be set apart to bring glory to Him as a response.

Further Study:
Hebrews 2:3
Hebrews 5:9

E) He Remembered the Lord

But Jonah remembered the Lord! He knew his God, His personality, His characteristics, His emotions, His affections and His nature and as a result was brought back to his senses in seeing full well the foolishness of his ways. Oh how foolish the ways of any human being to defy this God of ours. How beautiful and glorious He is and yet multitudes choose their own ways. It is simply because they have not seen Him and do not know Him! One who has tasted of God will never, ever forget. They may falter for a season but will surely rise up after a time as Jonah did and "remember the Lord!" May we meditate on and behold our great King day in and day out in order to know Him in a greater capacity.

Further Study:
Philippians 3:10
Hebrews 6:4-6
John 4:10-14

F) God's Loving Discipline

Jonah, in verse 9, commits to do what he had run from in the first place. It is a time of rededication to obedience unto the Lord and to follow Him wherever He may lead. It is only after Jonah did this act of the will and it is truly solidified in his heart, that the fish spits Jonah out. It is an immediate act. The prison God had prepared served its end - to give Jonah time to repent and come back in line with God's ways and purpose. God was orchestrating nature to accomplish His grand purpose and would not allow the affliction to go on one minute longer than necessary. This is always the heart of God. He must discipline us and desires to as a loving Father. In doing so He seeks to bring us back in line with His heart. Once we have responded and surrendered ourselves afresh into His loving embrace and will, He will let up and bring us out of the fire of affliction.

➤ What might you need to do to rededicate yourself before the Lord?

➤ Is there some calling, some promise, some prophetic confirmation which over time has been set on the back burner? How will you move it back to the forefront?

➤ Is there something you've left undone that needed to be done? Set your face before the Lord to do this thing.

G)   A Forerunner of Christ

Jonah's time in the fish is to be seen as a picture of the resurrection of Jesus. God prepared the way and willed that Christ must die and bear the weight upon Himself of all of humanity's waywardness. Jesus needed to be crushed and go into the prison of death and dwell there three days and nights in order to set the captives free from eternal guilt and condemnation due to sin's power. He was then raised up again as death could not hold Him down and was resurrected with a glorified, physical body on the third day. Jonah's very real experience is a type and a forerunner of Jesus' history-altering sacrifice and subsequent resurrection.

Further Study:

Matthew 12:40
Isaiah 53:10

The Book of Jonah – Passage 7

Read Jonah 3:1-3 - Obeying God's Call

God speaks a second time to Jonah to go to Nineveh. This time the prophet responds in obedience and follows the Lord's call to the great city.

A)   The God of Second Chances

God is the God of second chances….and third and fourth and so on. To those whose hearts are bent sincerely toward seeking Him and being known by Him deep in the inner man, though they may falter time after time, He gives more and more opportunities to get it right. God knows the difference, at a heart level, between open rebellion and disobedience based on weakness and misunderstanding.

If we are willing, He will discipline us from our misunderstanding and correct our low thinking, aligning it with His own. Open rebellion, on the other hand, marks us for judgment as we will not be deterred even though the Lord may lovingly try to coax us back through His caring hand. Jonah's experience was not outright punishment on the Lord's part, but correction of His wayward prophet.

<u>Reflection Questions:</u>

➢ Remember a time when the Lord clearly gave you a second and third and fourth chance to get something right.
➢ What did this do for your heart?
➢ Was a sense of confidence in the Lord and His absolute goodness seared into your spirit?

<u>Prayer:</u>
Jesus, I praise and thank you for being the God of second chances and more. I know I consistently need Your forgiveness and that You are committed to bringing restoration to me as I come humbly before you in complete surrender. I want to follow You with all of my heart and live faithfully for Your purposes and glory alone. Empower toward this end!

B)   No Waiting Period

In this section, God has reconciled Himself with His servant. The disobedience did not disqualify Jonah from His calling as God's Message Bearer. God had heard Jonah's cry in the belly of the fish, restored Jonah to Himself in fullness and now called him back to his original task.

How often we want to put ourselves aside when we know we have sinned against God. We want to add to God's discipline by putting ourselves into a period (hour, day, week, month, year, etc) to "pay" for our sin. Here, God shows that His grace is wholly sufficient and that restoration and total forgiveness, once granted by God, are the only needed things. We can't, nor should we deceive ourselves by trying, add anything else to His work through the cross. Doing so is idolatry and trusting in self and not Christ's blood alone. Jonah is immediately commissioned by God back to his original task.

Reflection Question:

➤ Recall a time when you had sinned and following repentance still felt like you needed to stay on the sideline for a while. This is so common yet not the heart of Jesus at all.
➤ What would you do differently next time to get back in the game immediately?

C) A Picture of Wholehearted Consecration

Jonah arose with a willingness to obey God's Word this time. This is the picture of the yielded, submitted and cheerful servant and representative of Jesus Christ. He did not put his own plans and desires first, but was now living in complete consecration to God's will and plans. Jonah had learned the first great lesson of the book through the gracious correction of God Most High.

We will also experience many corrections of the Lord as He molds us, forms us, conforms us to His image and into the Message Bearers He has commissioned us to be in this hour of human history. The only question is how will we respond to such corrections? Will we even recognize them as being from the hand of the Lord in the first place? We need to ask the Lord for greater discernment, wisdom and perspective to know when it is He that is correcting us through various circumstances, when such things are fruit of our own doing or even from the enemy seeking to derail us.

Prayer:
Lord, like Jonah I want to arise boldly after falling and commit myself wholeheartedly to Your purposes. I forsake all of my own plans and desires and choose to make Your will my will. Thank you for correcting me and teaching me of Your kindness. Give me greater spiritual wisdom, understanding and perspective to see Your ways and to go after them with all my heart.

D) The Witness of the Word and Spirit

God spoke clearly the second time – "Preach against Nineveh the message I tell you." The public declaring of the Word of God is central to bringing forth conviction in the heart of people. The Holy Spirit powerfully accompanies the declaration of God's Holy Word. It is the Witness against people's hearts and minds. There was more, however, that the Lord had to say to the Ninevites than what He called for in Jonah 1:2. It was the call to be ready for the unveiling of prophetic revelation in communicating to the Ninevites.

With us it is the same. God has given us His written Word to declare and proclaim as a Witness. Yet we are also called to live by the Spirit in response to specific details He might want to communicate in a specific situation to draw the hearer more to Himself. Message Bearers who are most effective in being used by the Spirit to bring forth conviction in people's hearts marry the Word and the Spirit's particular revelation in a situation. Only God's written Word is infallible while our ability to rightly interpret His voice at times falls horribly short of this. This doesn't mean we should not continue to seek to function in this reality, however. The Bible tells us that the letter itself kills but it is the Spirit that gives life. The two flowing together and fully complementing and aligning with each other is how God has always intended to bring forth the greatest amount of fruit possible.

Further Study:
Matthew 24:14
Luke 21:12-19
Ephesians 1:17-20

E)   God's Big Stage

We can only respond with awe as we grasp how truly large the city of Nineveh was. This is essential to rightly appreciate what is about to come. The city was much bigger than Babylon itself. It took three days to walk from one end of it to the other. It was massive for the ancient world. This context was the Parish in which God had called Jonah to declare, proclaim and prophesy against. The duty of preaching God's Word in such a place and the power of watching repentance break out in such a city was extraordinary.

When God wants to show Himself strong, He does so on the biggest stage He can find. We are to see in this His plans for today to break out in power in some of the seemingly most difficult places in the world. We are meant to be stirred in faith to believe Him for the "impossible" in our finite views. Nobody would have thought that the great city of Nineveh would ever repent and turn to the Lord. This was truly a miracle and wonder of the highest proportions. He wants us to trust that in the days to come, similar wonders are going to take place in great cities simply because of God's great love and kindness for people.

Modern South Korea is such a story. Just sixty years ago it was a nation of pagan idol worship with very few Christians. Now over 35% percent of the nation's population are sincere, born again believers. South Korea now boasts the highest percentage per capita of sent Message Bearers globally.

Further Study:
Luke 1:37
Matthew 17:20
Hebrews 11:6

F) Putting His Hand to the Plow

As Jonah enters the city, he immediately commences his commission from the Lord. In doing so, there is no hesitation, no assessing the situation, no surveying what might need to be done, no resting before the task, no turning back. With all boldness, courage, faith and trust in His God Jonah does according to all God had called him. This is a powerful example for us. Though such assessing, etc is not necessarily bad in itself, there are times when we simply need to urgently move with God and be faithful. These are times when He has shown Himself and His plans to us in a myriad of ways, making His will clear and now the ball falls entirely in our court. It is our turn to move with Him according to His purposes without any hesitation.

The Book of Jonah – Passage 8

Read Jonah 3:4-10 - Nineveh Hears and Dramatically Responds

Jonah enters the city and begins his ministry. The city responds dramatically and embraces repentance, proclaims a fast from the very least to the very greatest among them. The King of Nineveh himself declares a call to repentance to see if God might turn and not destroy them in His deserved wrath and anger. God does see their repentance and relents in bringing judgment and wholesale destruction. Based on His immense grace, God relents from His original plan.

A) The Power of God to Transform a City

Jonah's words were filled with coming judgment and destruction. Though Nineveh is a great and mighty city, violent and capable of defending itself, the Spirit of God moved on the hearts of the people of the whole city. They believed the Word, though every natural thing would have led them to reject it in their pride.

God is able to break the most hard-hearted of sinners, if we will be faithful to preach His Words, His ways, His commandments and be led by the Spirit. Entire cities are capable of turning to God, but the pure Word is the only thing that can accomplish this. This heathen city turned to God because of Jonah boldly and without compromise preaching the unpopular message of God's heart and love. We cannot substitute our politically correct, soft and gentle preaching for God's unshakable Word of Truth. In this hour when "truth" around the world is under severe attack, it is imperative that the people of God hold fast and arise with boldness motivated by extraordinary love.

Reflection Question:

➤ Can you envision what it might look like today to see an entire city brought to Jesus Christ? Ask the Lord to stir you with faith to believe Him for what seems impossible. Ask Him to put a specific unreached city on your heart to pray for.

B) The Coming Global Harvest

Isaiah 43: 4-11 paints a picture for us of what is to come as we near the end of the age. This is a Biblical prophecy that has multitudes of layers. As with much Biblical prophecy there is a near fulfillment and a distant fulfillment and many other lesser fulfillments in between. In the near future the fulfillment of this prophetic declaration was the ending of the Babylonian captivity and the freeing of the Israelites. The broader and much larger primary fulfillment has not yet taken place. It is a clear reference to a mighty revival that will sweep through the nations and draw an innumerable multitude of people into the Kingdom of Christ. It also is clear that this will happen prior to the Second Coming of Jesus and that we are to proactively believe and trust in this coming fulfillment.

What was taking place among the Ninevites was a confirmation that God indeed has the capacity to bring a monumental turning of hearts to pass. This is a small token for us to cling to as we purposefully wait upon God to bring forth His broader promise. We are meant to have our hearts bolstered with faith and confidence to trust Him and work together with Him in seeing the coming global harvest realized. This is meant to encourage us while we continue to serve God in the midst of often difficult circumstances.

Such a harvest will come to pass as God's Message Bearers offer themselves up in sacrifice for a particular people group. Because of the preciousness of God's people in His sight and because of His great affections and love for those who have said "Yes" to His Son, He will exchange our lives for the sake of multitudes who are currently lost and bring them into His Kingdom in a glorious manner.

Further Study:
Isaiah 43:4-11
Isaiah 49:1-13

C) Proclaiming the Superiority of God

God is displayed in Jonah's proclamations as the ruler over all things, able to overthrow even the strongest governments and kings and bring sudden destruction on a great people. His characteristics and nature must be communicated as they truly are to those who have never heard of our Great God. He ever lives to be intricately involved in the details of the lives of these precious ones. He longs to be represented and displayed as greater in every way then whatever false god the particular people is living for and serving. Nineveh saw this clearly in Jonah's God and believed it wholeheartedly. In response they changed their lives, altered their schedules and rearranged their priorities. The genuineness and sincerity of repentance is evidenced by radically adjusting things in order to make them right with God. We are to see in the Ninevite's radical response that all that matters is getting things right with God. The utmost calamity as human beings is to be out of relationship with the Most High God.

Further Study:
Haggai 2:7
Luke 3:8

D) The Place of Fasting

Fasting was an important part of the Ninevites' "works of repentance." This phrase simply means that their repentance before God was accompanied by tangible action that bore witness to the change in their heart. Their commitment to transformation was accompanied by sacrificial action. The whole governing rule of the city called for it. It was appointed from the highest and most powerful of the city who until now had been openly hostile to this God and His people. This fasting had several critical elements to make it acceptable by God:

A) Prayer and mighty crying out to God in sorrow and remorse accompanied it. They sought God in recognition of their gross wickedness as being a total and complete affront to Him and His nature.

B) A change of heart was necessary - they were to turn from the evil of their ways. Action must always follow true repentance. Something must be done to reconcile or restore the sin repented of. A turning, with clear-cut accountable plans, is required for true repentance to be received by the Lord.

Reflection Question:

➤ Have you considered the place of fasting and its role in alleviating judgment? This is a very biblical concept and one that needs reinstating today.
➤ How will you use this teaching this week?

Further Study:
Joel 2

E) A Whole City Turned To God

It is astounding that this people known as being brutal, tortuous, taking pleasure in violence and filth, would so quickly turn. We are meant to understand by the text that literally the hearts of the whole city responded to God. God's power and extravagant love is big enough to accomplish this. We are to believe today that He is calling forth similar types of ministry among difficult cities and people groups. He is provoking His Message Bearers, many of whom are going to very hostile and godless places and peoples in the earth, to proclaim in word and deed the unhindered and uncompromised Word of God. Such proclamation will indeed bring forth fruit that remains for His glory.

F) "Who Can Tell...?"

The reason behind the decree of the King is clarified in verse. 9. *"Who can tell if God will turn and relent?"* God's relenting was not a final conclusion and the King knew this. They did not know what God would do and if He would indeed relent from His initial purpose of bringing destruction upon them. Would such a dramatic response of a whole city, under God's divine wrath, move Him to relent?

It is the same today. God's divine wrath is being kindled today in many cities around the earth as they are filled with increasing wickedness and blatant opposition to God and His Kingdom. His justice dictates that destruction must come to pay for such waywardness. Yet, will He relent in bringing destruction if these give themselves to the great reversal through true, sincere repentance? We never know if this will be so. We are not talking about individual salvation here, as we understand that is assured if we put our faith in Christ. We do know that He will forgive sin and justify by His blood. Yet, avoiding a potential judgment in the here and now is another matter. Our role is to faithfully call people to repentance and show them how to receive Jesus' finished work, in order to avert His justified fury against them.

<u>Reflection Questions:</u>

➤ Reflect on what the above comment means to you.

➤ What might it mean for your response to the Lord and your understanding of His calling on your life?

G)   Nineveh's Response and God's Subsequent Relenting

The Ninevites' response is incredible! Because of Jonah's clear and articulate proclamation that God was against them in their wickedness, they now are aware that they deserve God's fierce anger and judgment as they have been an exceedingly wicked people. They seek no other higher court, knowing that God's declaration, either against them or possibly now for them as they have turned to Him, is the final one. Their only hope is for God to relent and have mercy upon them.

How easily we fail to cast our own hope upon the Lord in such a way. We cling to side issues and may claim a commitment to Jesus, yet often fail to recognize Him as the great judge that He is. In this situation, God does relent from the disaster that was coming. Such a relenting was in response to the genuineness and sincerity of the Ninevite's forsaking their ways. It is only sincere repentance accompanied with action bearing witness to the thing repented of, which stays the hand of God. In His justice, God must judge sin and eventually destroy those who tolerate it.

The repentance of the Ninevites moved the heart of God to change the decree He had made against them. For many this can pose a theological problem. We know that God is omniscient and does not change. He knows the end from the beginning. His foreknowledge is complete. Yet, so often we find in the Old Testament the words, "the Lord repented" or changed his mind. Jonah's message of judgment was conditional on the people's response. God possesses laws in dealing with humanity. Sin requires judgment whereas true heart level repentance breeds His tender mercy. In such situations it can be said that people change, not God. People's change of heart with repentance makes it now morally possible for God to respond with mercy instead of the judgment He had intended to bring. In doing so, God is still acting completely consistent with His holy principles and character.

It is important to note that the Ninevites' repentance was sincere and real, but eventually forgotten, as they slid back into the evil of their ways. Nahum prophesies one hundred years later of the judgment against the Ninevites and the fulfillment of that prophetic declaration (book of Nahum). Their repentance did not pass down to the succeeding generations.

The Book of Jonah – Passage 9

Read Jonah 4:1-4 - The Need For a Paradigm Shift

Jonah's negative response here seems misplaced. The events taking place among the Ninevites (their turning from evil and God's relenting) angered him. He knew God, His nature, His characteristics and His ways and his prayer reveals the crux of his previous disobedience. In a word Jonah hated Nineveh and its people. He did not want them spared of God's wrath. He knew their violence, wickedness, cruelty and abominations and of their previous merciless attacks upon the Israelites.

A)   God's Call To Single-Mindedness

God's Message Bearers are called to obedience, even when our opinions, emotions or personal will seem to stand in the way. His divine purpose alone must be the overriding, all-consuming passion of our hearts, no matter our personal view of a people, a city, or any situation in our lives. This is a difficult lesson to learn as often we have been seriously hurt by the ones God may now be asking us to respond to and serve. It is in such a calling that we are privileged to cling to the fact that truly our lives are not about seeking our own dreams or desires. Instead we are to single-mindedly seek bringing glory to the One we so dearly love. Such obedience will forever substantiate the great gulf between our true home in heaven and our brief period of time on this earth.

Reflection Questions:

➢   Would you agree that it is your single most important desire presently to bring Jesus the greatest amount of glory possible? If not, what might you need to adjust or get rid of in your life in order to more align yourself with such a purpose?

Further Study:
1 Samuel 15:22
2 Chronicles 30:12
Acts 5:29

B)   An Unspoken Reality Today

In our fallen human nature we can sympathize with Jonah. This people, like so many in our own day, are cruel and they seem to deserve God's wrath and judgment. Deep down we also hate them (though this would never be stated consciously). Though we know God and love Him, it is quite difficult to bring ourselves to love these people enough to do whatever it takes to see them given the opportunity to be brought into Jesus' Kingdom. To give ourselves as His Message Bearers seems to cost so much and these people don't really seem to be worth it to us. Obviously, none of these feelings, thoughts or realities are verbalized in this way or often even known by an individual. Often we deceive even ourselves with nice words and sentiments that we know are accepted in the Church. Yet when we're honest and willing to let the truth be known we struggle in this way.

We don't overcome this reality by ignoring it or acting as if we really do love these people to impress others or because we know it's what we're supposed to do as a follower of Jesus. We overcome it by simply aligning our hearts, over and over again, with God's own heart even when it is very hard to do so. We posture our hearts and lives to obey the commands of Christ, no matter the feelings, emotions or desires in our own heart for such a thing. We respond not so much with love for them but with love for our God, who has called us. Those whom God calls He will also provide with everything including feelings and emotions in time. This was what Jonah did. Such feelings will usually not be there initially but deep love will eventually follow the act of our will.

Reflection Questions:

➢ Where do you identify with such an unspoken reality in your own heart?
➢ What may God be asking you to do in order to overcome such an unspoken reality in your heart?

Further Study:
Jeremiah 17:9
1 Peter 1:3
Psalm 7:9

C)   Betraying Our Spiritual State

Yet Jonah's response as well as our own betrays much of the spiritual state of our lives that must be considered and dealt with before the Lord. (1) Jonah's displeasure and anger made clear his lack of rule over his own spirit. His was thus a city broken down internally (Proverbs 25:28). (2) His responses show his lack of reverence and fear of God. Though we can't always understand or grasp God's ways we are called to always yield ourselves to His sovereign wisdom. Jonah was confronted with a clear and evident move of God. When also confronted by such, our only response is to submit to the truth that He has indeed intervened and praise Him with great delight for such an act.

Further Study:
Proverbs 16:32
Psalm 9:1-2

D) Exposing Our Offenses

Mostly Jonah was jealous for his country and what would come of it now that Israel's enemies had been spared. His heart was hot over such a situation and was offended that God would allow such a thing. He prays a prayer- not a yielded prayer as he had in affliction within the fish's belly, but instead in angry passion.

Offense at God for something that He does or allows is common in the body of Christ today as well. It is often God's intent to offend our minds in order to reveal to us the real state of our hearts. An exposing of some offense deep within reveals that the particular area is not fully submitted to the Lordship of Jesus Christ in our lives. Such exposure is the grace of God toward us to help us overcome the particular area of weakness and to fully surrender it to Him, trusting in His vast wisdom.

Reflection Questions:

➤ Consider a time when you felt "offended" at God because of something He did which did not coincide with your understanding of Him. How did you deal with such a thought or feeling?

Further Study:
Matthew 11:1-6
Matthew 13:57

E) Jonah's Justification

Jonah justifies himself before the Lord by saying in effect, "See God, I knew this would happen because I know your character" - as if his own outlook actually had merit to it. It was a thoroughly wrong attitude. Unlike the other Biblical prophets, Jonah actually desired the horrifying day to come that he had prophesied. How often we know not of what spirit we are. We justify our hatred by the actions and wickedness of others. Jonah possessed a strong root of bitterness that had not been stripped away and he continued to indulge it. It is to our advantage to invite the Holy Spirit to deal with such deep seated biases.

Reflection Question:

➤ Who has hurt you in such a way that you find it difficult to think about that person receiving the blessing of God? What will you do to reverse this thinking?

Further Study:
Hebrews 12:15
Deuteronomy 29:18
Luke 9:54-55

F)   The Message Bearer God in Action

Next, Jonah wishes for death. Jonah asks God to take him out of this life because of his personal despair over God's merciful dealings with these people. In essence he says, "If Nineveh must live, let me die! I don't want to see the glory of Israel given to the Gentiles." He was jealous for God to keep His love, grace and favor only for His chosen people, Israel. The first century church had to face a similar crisis when God threw open the gates of His Kingdom to the Gentiles. God is a missionary God in every sense and the book of Jonah is the first instance that we clearly see this in action. It is a precursor of what is to come through the death and resurrection of Jesus Christ and the worldwide expansion of the Gospel being instituted.

Reflection Questions:

➤ Have you grasped the reality that God is a missionary God in every way?
➤ How might you need to alter your priorities in order to align yourself with such a reality?

Further Study:

Acts 10:9-16
Matthew 28:18-20
1 John 2:2

G)   Jonah's Self-Pity

God used Jonah powerfully. He should have been considering if he should continue this highly fruitful outreach to the other cities of Assyria. Instead, in self-pity, he is considering death. His relationship with God, at this point, is again strained as it had been earlier in the book. To come before the judgment seat of Christ having willingly, out of personal offense, turned his heart from God, was not wisdom. How often we allow self-pity to dominate our hearts and minds before the Lord. We justify ourselves into thinking that we actually live for ourselves instead of the reality that we are Jesus' bond-slaves.

Reflection Question:

➤ Self-pity is extremely dangerous to our spiritual lives. In what ways have you allowed yourself to get down or discouraged based on self-pity?

Further Study:

Philippians 2:7
1 Corinthians 6:20
1 Corinthians 7:23

H)   The Key Lesson of the Book – Stop Exclusiveness

The Lord, in His grace calls Jonah back to his spiritual senses by saying, "Is it right for you to be angry?" He could have killed him right there for such a hotheaded response, yet God, rich in mercy, seeks to walk His servant through the wrong attitudes. God is ever seeking to teach us, reprove us, correct us, mold us in order to form us more and more with His heart and perspective in every situation. In this situation, God is teaching the major lesson of the entire book - an overcoming of the sin of the exclusiveness of the Israelites. This is the sin of imagining that the light we've received from God is somehow for us alone and not for others.

<u>Further Study:</u>

1 Peter 2:9
Ephesians 5:8-10
Acts 26:17-18
1 John 2:2

The Book of Jonah – Passage 10

Read Jonah 4:5-11 - God's Great Object Lesson

After this exchange with the Lord, Jonah leaves the city and goes outside the gates. He makes a place to rest and waits to see what will happen to the city. The Lord prepares a bush, which protects Jonah and then quickly raises up a worm to eat the bush. Next God prepares a wind to blow, making it quite hot which causes Jonah to almost faint. All this He does as an object lesson to teach Jonah, molding his paradigm and changing his heart.

A) The Risk

Jonah risks much with his hasty departure from the city. As the carrier of the message, the Ninevites' would have been ready to treat Jonah with great honor. Such a seemingly rash and culturally inappropriate response on his part would have been seen as disrespectful, maybe even a mockery to them. In this way Jonah could have potentially caused great injury to the very message he had brought. The fact that this didn't happen shows us something important about what was taking place among the people. The power and work of God was the focus for the Ninevites' and not the charisma or abilities of the messenger. It is important that as Message Bearers we put all of the emphasis on the Lord and never focus on ourselves. His power must be displayed and His honor and glory worshipped.

Further Study:

1 Corinthians 2:4-5
John 3:30

B) The Kind and Tender Provider

Jonah then finds himself outside of the gate with no shelter. Yet God in His rich kindness and generosity brings Jonah a provision. God knows His prophet is disheartened and He seeks to help alleviate some of Jonah's pain. God is so consumed with compassion for His people. His tenderness for us as we struggle with affliction (even when we bring it upon ourselves as Jonah did here) is great. It is God who prepares and sovereignly raises up the plant even though Jonah had fled the scene in disgust and anger. Inside the city gates Jonah had adequate shelter. God is intimately involved in all that we do and with caring for our perfect provision. He, at times, will even supply for us when we wrongly flee a situation because of an offense in our own hearts.

Further Study:
Philippians 4:19
Psalm 138:8

C) A Caution About Comforts

The plant turned out to be a great comfort to Jonah. His heart was encouraged and soothed by it. Maybe too much so! He seems to have taken pride in it and gloried in it. Comforts are good and we are to give thanks to the Lord for them in their moderation, yet we should never be exceedingly joyful over them. God alone is our exceedingly great reward. As a result of Jonah's response to the plant, the Lord takes the plant away from him. When our treasure is in anything besides Jesus, God will orchestrate situations to help motivate us to move away from such things. God is jealous for our wholesale affection for Christ and as a result wants us holding lightly to all else.

Such taking of the plant came not by chance but by direct command of God. Just as He had raised up the plant, God now raises up a worm to destroy it. This was all done in order to teach Jonah not to take too much joy and comfort in things made to be refreshing and beneficial to us. Comforts come for a time and if trusted in too much, soon may be cut down. If we trust in them we will always be disappointed as they can never deeply satisfy us. Our hearts were never meant to find a home in such things. Yet in our weak flesh we seem to seek them constantly nonetheless.

Reflection Question:

➤ What particular comforts are there in your life that may be too much of an attachment to you right now?
➤ What will you do about them today?

Further Study:
Luke 12:34

D) Ungoverned Emotions

God then brought the heat that caused Jonah to nearly faint. Jonah then, for a second time, asks God that he may die. Jonah had given into a spirit of grumbling and complaining similar to the Israelites in the wilderness during the Exodus. God rebukes Jonah a second time for his misplaced anger. In response Jonah again seeks to justify himself stating that he has reason to be angry.

Much of Jonah's downfall centered around his extreme passions. Jonah was a man given to emotionalism which clouded his clarity of thought and rationalism. It sometimes did the same with Peter in the New Testament and it does the same with us. This emotionalism sidetracked Jonah initially from going to the Ninevites when God commanded him, and now in trusting in the plant too much. Jonah possessed inordinate affections that were not balanced or governed by his spirit.

There is a good way to tell if our emotions are out of balance. If we are overly enthused by certain circumstances or we highly rejoice over positive situations in an extreme fashion we will conversely be found to swing to the other side of extreme grief when such things are taken away from us. God desires that our emotions be governed and balanced. Jonah is to be a negative model to us of ungoverned emotions.

<u>Reflection Question:</u>

- ➢ Have you found it true in your life that you often times have ungoverned emotions? Inordinate affections for certain things?
- ➢ What effect does this have on your life?

E) God's Overwhelming Love For All Humanity

God's response to Jonah is to compare Jonah's love for the plant which Jonah has now lost with His own for the wicked Ninevites. Jonah had pity on this solitary plant yet God's pity was for a population of about 600,000. Jonah's plant was not his own. He had done nothing to create the plant or make it rise up. He had only enjoyed the benefits of it. God, on the other hand, had created and loved these people since before the foundation of the world. Yet, they did not know anything about Him. They were the work of His own hands, His beloved ones whom He had breathed life into. He was the author of their lives and the One who preserves and sees them through and through.

If one soul is of great value to the Lord, how much more are 600,000? Jonah had pity on a plant yet God had much more justification in pitying the Ninevites', who were living in complete spiritual darkness. We must grasp the deep concern of our Father for every human being who is currently outside of a relevant hearing of the Gospel of Christ. As we consider Jonah's inordinate affections for this plant in comparison with God's monumental love for all humanity, we are to marvel at our own low thinking and love for petty comforts. Such keep the Church from sacrificially moving forward with greater momentum and fervency to complete the Great Commission in our lifetime.

<u>Further Study:</u>
1 John 2:2
Revelation 12:9

Post Thought

Though the book ends on a negative note for Jonah, we can be satisfied that he comprehended the lessons God was seeking to teach him. Jonah wrote this book as is, putting himself in a negative light by doing so. Jonah's humility shines forth as he seeks to use his own experience to teach the people of God, for all time, the key lessons he had learned and to grow in our understanding and love for the great God He served. The book of Jonah screams aloud "don't make the same mistakes I made, but learn from my experience and allow the Lord to cultivate His own passion and love for all peoples deep within you!"

Conclusion

I trust that the Lord has used these studies in Jonah to open your eyes to some of the ways of God in forming His people. As I have given myself to study Jonah over the years my heart is consistently awed and astounded at the greatness of God as He relates with us, His precious children.

Let us consider again the main reasons why we seek to study the book of Jonah. Consider what the Lord has been doing very specifically to help you grasp and internalize these truths. (1) About More Than a Fish – the intent of Jonah's story is to remove our wrong ways of viewing God, His church and the world. (2) Jonah – The Test Book of the Bible - Everything in the book demands that we believe in the Supernatural God and trust His Word literally and implicitly. (3) The Two-Fold Purpose of God - We find in the book of Jonah a clear presentation of the two highest priorities in the heart of God. (4) Implementing a Dramatic Paradigm Shift - In Jonah we find a representation of the common attitude of pride surrounding being God's chosen people. (5) Understanding God's Message Bearer Heart - The book of Jonah is meant to teach the body of Christ today the absolute inclusiveness of God's Kingdom through Jesus Christ and to rebuke our propensity and attitude of being an exclusive people. (6) Understanding the Ways of God in Shaping His People - We study Jonah in order to be aware of the sovereign hand of God moving and teaching us through potentially similar means. (7) Jonah – A Type of Israel - We see Jonah as a representation of Israel.

God is doing something profound in the earth today. He has a deliberate purpose of revealing hope and love en masse and to see that all people groups are given an opportunity to respond to His grace and kindness. At the core of the book of Jonah is this heart of love for all humanity stuck in the mire of sin. Yet the narrative surrounds a follower of God who, out of his own selfish opinions and priorities, does not want to align with God's desires. We are meant to see our own tendencies to shun the desires and purposes of God instead of rightly giving ourselves fully over to Him as our great King and Lord. Have you allowed the Lord to begin the process of ridding you of some of these same wrong outlooks? I trust that as you have sought the Lord through these studies, such a process has begun in your heart.

If you have sensed the leading of the Holy Spirit in your life through these studies to potentially state your intentions to become a message bearer of God's great love among the unreached, let me encourage you to visit www.GlobalMMI.net and sign the Go Declaration. By doing so, you join a fellowship of your peers from around the world who are also making the same commitment before the Lord. God is raising up a company of wholehearted and devoted believers to take His gospel to those in desperate need of it today. Join the movement today!

GLOBAL
MISSION
MOBILIZATION
INITIATIVE

"The Lausanne Committee for World Evangelization enthusiastically affirms the work and vision of GMMI. GMMI's commitment to mobilizing & equipping the global church toward its role in the task of reaching the world for Christ is compelling and strategic."

GlobalMMI.net / info@GlobalMMI.net

>>> **Who We Are:** We are a growing global mission mobilization initiative multiplying national mission mobilization movements mobilizing and equipping local ministries and disciples at every level of the body of Christ.

>>> **What We Do:** We multiply mission mobilization movements globally in three primary ways:

1. An international step by step strategy multiplying mission mobilization movements at every ministry level across a national church
2. A *Great Commission Equipping Center (GCEC)* in Chiang Mai, Thailand
3. A publishing arm, *IGNITE Media*, producing high quality mission mobilization and equipping materials and resources.

>>> **Core Objectives:**

1. Movements of individual disciples mobilized and equipped for Jesus' Great Commission
2. Movements of individual local ministries mobilized and equipped for Jesus' Great Commission
3. Movements of individual denominations and church organizations mobilized and equipped for Jesus' Great Commission
4. Movements of national evangelical alliances and associations in every nation mobilized and equipped for Jesus' Great Commission

More IGNITE Media Resources

IGNITE Media is the publishing arm of GMMI. Books, booklets, bible studies, DVD's, blogs and more are produced to serve your ministry in deepening the spiritual life and mobilizing and equipping for cross-cultural mission. Visit http://www.globalmmi.net/resources/

Cultivating Abandoned Devotion to Jesus

God is calling His people into deeper relationship with Himself. This is the beginning of all effective ministry and the only way effective ministry is continuously sustained. We cultivate this wholeheartedness through studying His Word deeply while applying all we are learning. These Bible studies go deep into the heart of God's Word, revealing depths and insight that will revolutionize your spiritual life. These can be used individually or in a group setting.

Studies in the Life of Joseph

Studies in the Book of Jonah

Studies in the Book of Colossians

Studies in the Sermon on the Mount

Studies in Jesus' Parables of the Kingdom

Studies in the Seven Churches of Revelation

Studies in Matthew 24-25

Mobilizing Local Ministries

The Holy Spirit is raising a vision of not merely one by one mission mobilization, but the concept of mobilizing and equipping whole local ministries for Jesus' Great Commission. These resources enable that process through the use of proven tools and teaching. Each of these resources serve a unique purpose toward seeing disciples mobilized and equipped through local ministries to serve the unreached.

Handbook for Great Commission Ministries (*English, Spanish, French, Chinese (both simplified and traditional), Thai*)
Great Commission Bible Studies
Global Prayer Teams
Six Roles in the Great Commission
Developing a Sending Strategy
Waking the Giant
Where's Your Haystack DVD

Equipping For Global Harvest

To see the literal fulfillment of the Great Commission we need to be equipped in particular areas often not discussed or emphasized. These resources provide focus on core areas of equipping the Holy Spirit is emphasizing and that need to be carefully grasped and integrated into our lives if we will be effective.

Engaging the Holy Spirit

Declare His Glory Among the Nations

Proclaiming the Kingdom

Spiritual Equipping For Mission

Deeper